AT THE END OF THE DAY

BY LUCY STUBBINGTON

First Published in 2025 by Blossom Spring Publishing
At The End Of The Day Copyright © 2025 Lucy Stubbington
ISBN 978-1-917938-27-3
E: admin@blossomspringpublishing.com
W: www.blossomspringpublishing.com
Lucy Stubbington as the author and Lucy Stubbington as the illustrator, have been asserted in accordance with the Copyright, Designs and Patents Act, 1988.
All rights reserved under international Copyright Law.
Contents and/or cover may not be reproduced in whole or in part without the express written consent of the publisher.

This book is dedicated to my very naughty,
but very handsome dog.
For you Paolo.

I love you in the garden,

When you're digging by the shed,

Even when you run inside,

And leave footprints on my bed!

I love you in the kitchen, sitting by my feet...

...Even when Mummy forgets to cover up the tasty treats!

Your paws padding on the ground,

Even when you roll in puddles,

And shake mud flying all around!

I love you when we're playing,

You always catch the ball!

I love you at the school gates...

Your deep bark that we all know!

Even when I run outside,
You jump up to say...

HELLO!

I love you at bathtime,

Even if you eat
 my socks,
  from the pile
   of dirty clothes!

I love you
at the end of the day,
when all is said
and done...

I'll see you in
the morning,

Lucy Stubbington was born in Hampshire in England.
She graduated with a BA(Hons) degree in illustration from Falmouth University in Cornwall. Since leaving Falmouth, Lucy has worked within the Illustration industry covering editorial articles, creating her own brand of homeware design and carrying out private commisions.

As a mother of her two young children, Lucy takes much inspiration for her illustration and children's book writing from their chaotic yet loving family environment. Spending time playing, talking to her little girls and exploring young imaginations ignites wonderful ideas that Lucy enjoys developing through words and paint. Eventually evolving into published stories.

Lucy also runs a cafe in her local village. She finds meeting many walks of life another fantastic way to create new illustrations and ideas for young readers. She loves creating good honest food for her customers as well as her family and friends.

Lucy enjoys spending time with her little family, seeking adventures big and small with their big black labrador in tow!

Lucy's website can be found at www.arosylife.co.uk

www.blossomspringpublishing.com